D1269165

Beagles

ABDO
Publishing Company

A Buddy Book
by
Julie Murray

VISIT US AT
www.abdopub.com

Published by Buddy Books, an imprint of ABDO Publishing Company, 4940 Viking Drive, Suite 622, Edina, Minnesota 55435. Copyright © 2002 by Abdo Consulting Group, Inc. International copyrights reserved in all countries. No part of this book may be reproduced in any form without written permission from the publisher.

Printed in the United States.

Edited by: Christy DeVillier
Contributing Editors: Matt Ray, Michael P. Goecke
Graphic Design: Maria Hosley
Image Research: Deborah Coldiron
Cover Photograph: Eyewire
Interior Photographs: American Kennel Club

Library of Congress Cataloging-in-Publication Data

Murray, Julie, 1969-
  Beagles/Julie Murray.
      p. cm. — (Animal kingdom)
  Summary: A brief introduction about a member of the hound family, which includes its history, physical characteristics, and proper care.
    ISBN 1-57765-643-1
    1. Beagle (Dog breed)—Juvenile literature. [1. Beagle (Dog breed) 2. Dogs. 3. Pets.] I. Title. II. Animal kingdom (Edina, Minn.)

SF429.B3 M86 2002
636.753'7—dc21

                                                                2001034930

Contents

Hound Dogs

Beagles are hound dogs. Hounds are good hunting dogs. Hunting dogs find their prey by scent. Beagles have a sharp sense of smell. This sharp sense of smell makes beagles great hunting dogs.

Beagles have a good sense of smell.

Beagles Long Ago

Long ago, the rulers of England hunted with beagles. Beagles helped hunters find hare, rabbits, and fox. Beagles would howl or bay when they smelled their prey. A bay is a long, singing bark. A howl is a high-pitched cry.

People hunt with beagles today.

Beagles have been around for a long time. These hounds lived more than 2,000 years ago in Greece.

Beagles have been around for thousands of years.

How Beagles Size Up

St. Bernard

Dalmatian

Beagle

Dachshund

What Beagles Look Like

Beagles are strong dogs for their size. Most beagles stand 10 to 15 inches (25.4 to 38.1 cm) tall at the shoulders. They can weigh up to 30 pounds (13.6 kg).

Beagles have long, floppy ears. A beagle carries its straight tail up high.

A beagle's coat is short, thick, and straight. The most common beagles are black, tan, and white. Many beagles today have all-black backs. We call these beagles "black blanketed."

long and floppy ears

straight tail carried high

Care

Beagles are good house pets. These dogs hardly ever bite. Beagles play well with children. But beagles need a lot of love and attention.

Keeping your beagle clean is easy. They do not need a lot of baths. You only need to brush your beagle once a week. Brushing your beagle's coat keeps it smooth and clean.

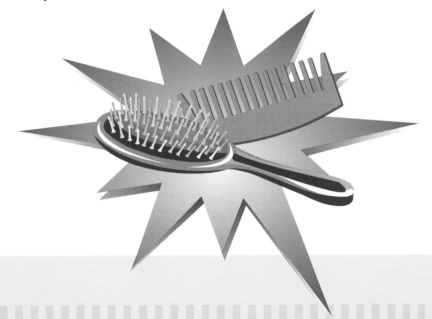

A beagle's sharp sense of smell will lead it away from home. So, do not let your beagle run free. Keep your beagle on a leash or in a fenced yard. A fenced yard is a great place to play with your dog.

All dogs need a good diet. Beagles are no different. A veterinarian can help you choose the best food for your beagle.

Beagles make great pets.

Puppies

Beagle puppies are born black and white or tan and white. A litter of beagles can have up to six puppies. Beagle puppies are born blind and deaf. They will begin to see and hear at about three weeks old. At eight weeks old, beagle puppies can leave their mother.

Playful beagle puppies.

Beagle Jobs

A beagle can find a lot with its sharp-smelling nose. So, people decided to give jobs to these hounds. Some beagles work in the Beagle Brigade. The Beagle Brigade smells fruit and meat entering the United States. They help the U.S. Department of Agriculture find bad food. Bad foods carrying disease or bugs cannot enter the U.S.

A member of the Beagle Brigade.

The Beagle Brigade works at airports and post offices, too. They sniff suitcases and boxes coming from different countries. They smell for things that should not be coming into America.

This hard-working beagle is sniffing suitcases.

The Beagle Brigade works at airports, too.

Important Words

brigade a group that works together.

hare an animal like a rabbit.

litter the group of puppies a dog has at one time.

prey an animal that is hunted by other animals.

scent smell.

veterinarian an animal doctor. A shorter name for veterinarian is "vet."

Web Sites

How to Love Your Dog

www.howtoloveyourdog.com
Facts about breeds, dog care advice, and riddles are featured here.

American Kennel Club

www.akc.org
Learn more about beagles and other dog breeds.

Animaland

www.animaland.org
Read about different kinds of pets at this fun site full of games, cartoons, and stories.

Index